DISNEY · PIXAR
THE INCREDIBLES
TOP 10s

NO GUTS,
NO GLORY

JENNIFER BOOTHROYD

LERNER PUBLICATIONS ◆ MINNEAPOLIS

Lerner Publications Company
A division of Lerner Publishing Group, Inc.
241 First Avenue North
Minneapolis, MN 55401 USA

For reading levels and more information, look up this title at
www.lernerbooks.com.

Main body text set in ITC Avant Garde Gothic 13/14.
Typeface provided by International Typeface Corp.

Library of Congress Cataloging-in-Publication Data

Names: Boothroyd, Jennifer, 1972– author.
Title: The Incredibles top 10s : no guts, no glory / Jennifer Boothroyd.
Description: Minneapolis : Lerner Publications, 2019. | Series: My top 10
    Disney | Includes bibliographical references and index. | Audience:
    Age 6–10. | Audience: K to Grade 3.
Identifiers: LCCN 2018011481 (print) | LCCN 2018012171 (ebook) |
    ISBN 9781541543621 (eb pdf) | ISBN 9781541539082 (lb : alk.
    paper)
Subjects: LCSH: Incredibles (Motion picture)—Juvenile literature.
Classification: LCC PN1997.2.I63 (ebook) | LCC PN1997.2.I63 B66 2019
    (print) | DDC 791.43/72—dc23

LC record available at https://lccn.loc.gov/2018011481

Manufactured in the United States of America
1-45091-35918-6/13/2018

TABLE OF CONTENTS

SUPER OPINIONS AND INCREDIBLE FACTS?

HEROES WITH SUPER POWERS ARE AMAZING, BUT A FAMILY OF SUPERS . . . THAT'S INCREDIBLE! There's so much to love about the Incredibles—their super powers, their high-tech gadgets, and the ways they catch the bad guys. But the best part is how they work together as a team.

The lists in this book highlight the ten best things about many parts of the Incredibles' world. Maybe you'll agree with these opinions. Maybe you won't. Maybe you'll want to change a list completely. That's fine. The important thing is to have fun on the adventure. Don't worry. You'll have a chance to give your opinions before you've finished this book.

SO ARE YOU READY TO JUMP INTO THE WORLD OF THE INCREDIBLES?

LET'S GO!

MR. INCREDIBLE'S TOP 10 INCREDIBLE MOMENTS

10 He breaks the rules to help the old woman with her insurance claim.

9 He rescues people from a burning building.

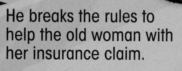
HE AND FROZONE MAKE IT LOOK EASY.

8 He breaks into the Tunneler to try to catch the Underminer.

7 He discovers the Omnidroid's weakness.

THE ONLY THING THAT CAN DAMAGE IT IS ITSELF.

6 He uses a train yard as an exercise gym.

5 He works underwater to turn a ship.

HE MUST HAVE SUPER LUNGS TO HOLD HIS BREATH THAT LONG!

4

He supports his wife's career by taking care of the kids.

"I'VE GOT TO SUCCEED, SO SHE CAN SUCCEED. SO WE CAN SUCCEED."

3 After an all-night study session, he finally figures out Dash's math homework.

2 He apologizes to Violet for not knowing how to help her with her crush.

HEY, SUPER DADS AREN'T PERFECT!

1 HE REALIZES HIS FAMILY MUST WORK TOGETHER TO DEFEAT SYNDROME.

TOP 10 FEATURES OF AN INCREDIBLE SUPERSUIT

10 Bulletproof material helps when you're battling bad guys.

BLAM!

9 It has a homing device.

GOOD IF YOU'VE BEEN CAPTURED. BAD IF YOU'RE SNEAKING AROUND A VILLAIN'S BASE.

8 It helps control Jack-Jack's morphing powers.

7 It's indestructible.

NOT EVEN A GARBAGE DISPOSAL CAN DESTROY IT.

6

It's made from a blend of high-tech materials and cotton.

THE COTTON IS FOR COMFORT.

∧ ∧ ∧ ∧ ∧
DID YOU KNOW?

Tailors make real-life clothing using paper patterns. The animators for the Incredibles movies started with patterns such as these to design the characters' clothing. Then a tailor helped the animators make digital patterns for the clothing in the movies.

5

It comes with a mask.

A SUPER'S SECRET IDENTITY IS THEIR MOST VALUABLE POSSESSION.

4

It protects from temps up to one thousand degrees.

3

It adapts to a Super's powers. Violet's Supersuit turns invisible. Elastigirl's stretches to match her shape.

2

Jack-Jack's new Supersuit has a fire extinguisher included.

BLACKBERRY-LAVENDER-FLAVORED FOAM, YUM!

1

IT'S MACHINE WASHABLE. CRIME FIGHTING IS A DIRTY JOB, AND SO IS LAUNDRY!

ELASTIGIRL'S TOP 10 INCREDIBLE MOMENTS

10 She uses her fighter-pilot skills to shake off incoming missiles.

9 She stretches to keep everyone in place at the dinner table.

8 When her leg gets stuck in a door, she stretches across two hallways and into a room to get the door's key.

SHE'S AS DETERMINED AS SHE IS FLEXIBLE!

7 She becomes a parachute to stop the runaway MetroLev train.

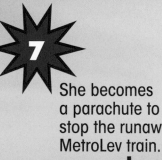

6 She drives the Elasticycle for the first time.

WHO KNEW THE HOUSE HAD A SECRET EXIT?

5 She flattens as thin as paper so she doesn't get squished by a train on Syndrome's island.

4 She changes her Elastigirl suit for an Incredibles suit.

THIS FAMILY WORKS BEST AS A TEAM!

3 When Syndrome kidnaps Jack-Jack, she has Mr. Incredible throw her into the air.

2 She discovers the Screenslaver's secret technology, the hypno-goggles.

TOO BAD THE SCREENSLAVER WAS NEXT TO HER WHEN SHE DID.

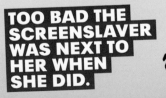

1 SHE SAVES EVERYONE IN THE CRASHING HELICOPTERS.

TOP 10 INCREDIBLES TECH

10

The Omnidroids learned how to battle Supers so well that one even figured out how to stop Syndrome.

THAT WAS DEFINITELY NOT PART OF SYNDROME'S EVIL PLAN.

9 The Tunneler helps the Underminer travel underground.

8 Syndrome's immobi-ray can stop people in their tracks and lift them off the ground.

7 With their spinning blades, you wouldn't want to get too close to a Velocipod.

BUT IT WOULD BE LOTS OF FUN TO FLY!

6 Elastigirl's Elasticycle gets her into the action quickly.

5 Not only does the Manta Jet fly, but it can also dive into water and transform into an underwater vehicle.

4 Hypno-goggles have the power to control people.

THANK GOODNESS THEY WERE DESTROYED!

3 Frozone's ice equipment transforms into skates, skis, and an ice disc whenever he needs it.

1

2 Edna's Jack-Jack monitor is pure genius.

THE CALMING OPTION IS A GAME CHANGER!

ROCKET THRUSTERS, AUTO-DRIVE, EJECTOR SEATS, A REMOTE CONTROL . . . THE INCREDIBILE HAS IT ALL!

VIOLET'S TOP 10 INCREDIBLE MOMENTS

10 She turns invisible when she sees Tony.

ARE YOU STILL BLUSHING IF NO ONE CAN SEE YOU?

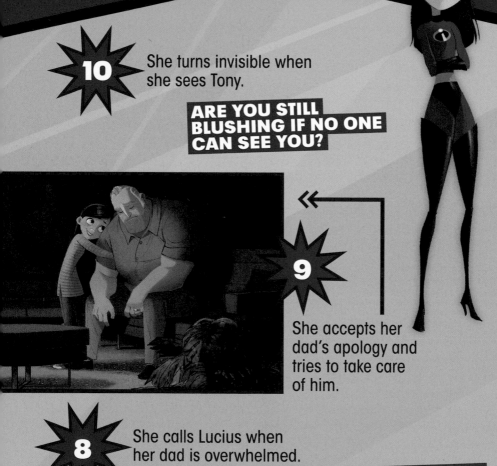

9 She accepts her dad's apology and tries to take care of him.

8 She calls Lucius when her dad is overwhelmed.

JACK-JACK IS A HANDFUL!

7 She protects everyone in the Tunneler before it explodes.

6

She questions her parents when they contradict themselves.

GROWING UP CAN BE CONFUSING.

∧∧∧∧∧
DID YOU KNOW?

In traditional animated movies, the creators draw a character's hair in a scene. When the character's hair moves, it's because an animator drew it to do so. But Violet's hair is simulated, not animated. A computer program controls how Violet's hair moves.

5

She uses *renounce* correctly in a sentence.

4

She creates a large force field for her and Dash to roll through the jungle.

JUST LIKE A HUGE HAMSTER BALL!

3

She fights off Voyd's attacks.

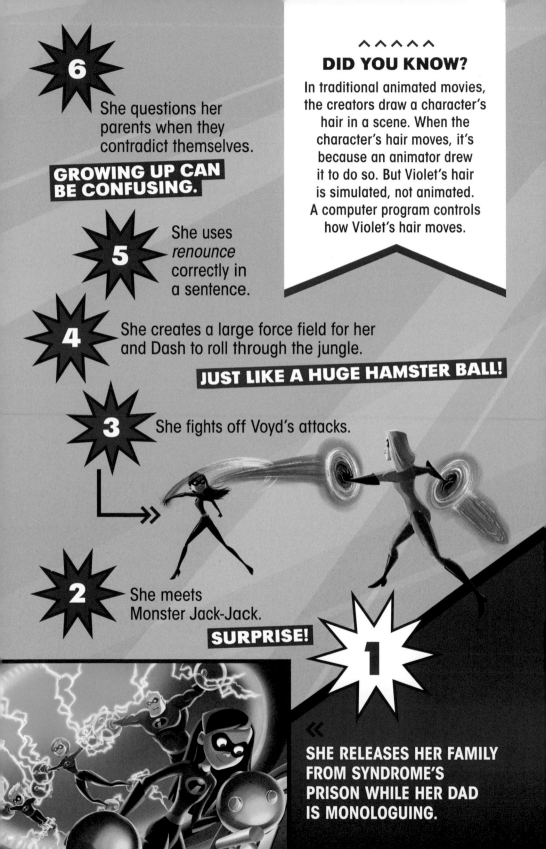

2

She meets Monster Jack-Jack.

SURPRISE!

1

« **SHE RELEASES HER FAMILY FROM SYNDROME'S PRISON WHILE HER DAD IS MONOLOGUING.**

TOP 10
INCREDIBLE LINES

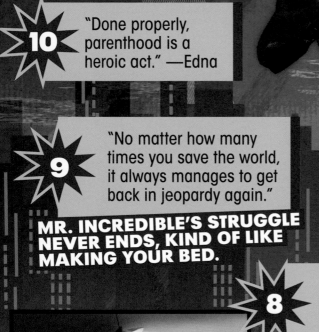

10 "Done properly, parenthood is a heroic act." —Edna

9 "No matter how many times you save the world, it always manages to get back in jeopardy again."

MR. INCREDIBLE'S STRUGGLE NEVER ENDS, KIND OF LIKE MAKING YOUR BED.

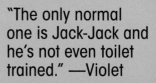

8 "I know what I *said*! Listen to what I'm saying now."

IT'S OKAY FOR A MOM TO CHANGE HER MIND.

7 "The only normal one is Jack-Jack and he's not even toilet trained." —Violet

6

"Is she having adolescence?"

DASH JUST CAN'T FIGURE OUT VIOLET.

∧ ∧ ∧ ∧ ∧
DID YOU KNOW?
Elastigirl uses real military flight terms when flying the jet to Syndrome's island.

5

"I'm used to knowing what the right thing to do is, but now I'm not sure anymore. I just want to be a good dad." —Mr. Incredible

4

"Where is my Supersuit?" —Frozone

3

"Why would they change math? Math is math!"

HAVE PATIENCE, MR. INCREDIBLE!

└─≫

2

"You know it's crazy, right? To help my family I gotta leave it; to fix the law, I gotta break it." —Elastigirl

1

WE ALL KNOW THIS ONE: "NO CAPES!" —EDNA

QUIZ BREAK!

Are you a superfan of the Incredibles? Take this quiz and find out!

1

WHY DOESN'T EVELYN LIKE SUPERS?

A Supers keep us weak.
B She is jealous of the Supers' powers.
C Supers are show-offs.
D She doesn't like people in masks.

2

WHAT COMPOSER DOES THE BABYSITTER PLAY FOR JACK-JACK?

A Beethoven
B Chopin
C Mozart
D Tchaikovsky

3

WHAT DOES EDNA USE TO PASS HER LAB SECURITY?

A Voice recognition
B Hand scan
C A secret code
D All of the above

4

WHAT IS THE NAME OF VIOLET'S CRUSH?

A Syndrome
B Brad Bird
C Tony Rydinger
D Rick Dicker

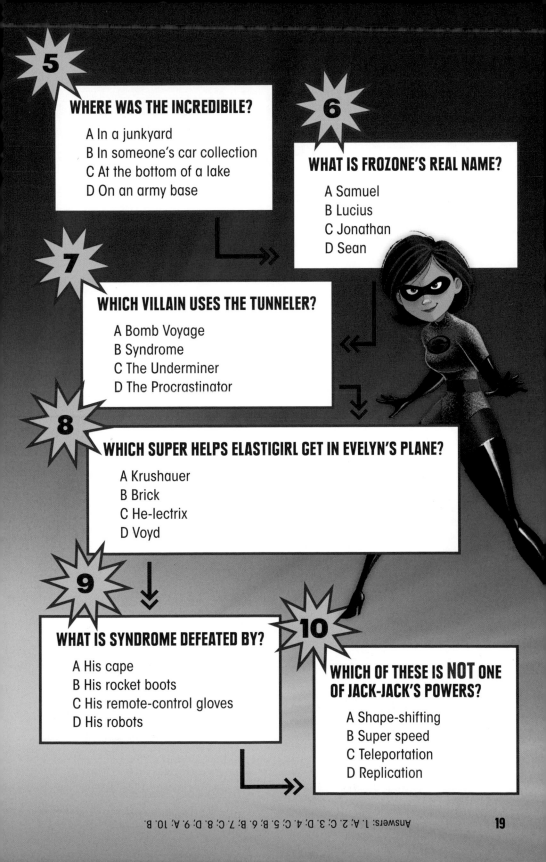

5

WHERE WAS THE INCREDIBILE?

A In a junkyard
B In someone's car collection
C At the bottom of a lake
D On an army base

6

WHAT IS FROZONE'S REAL NAME?

A Samuel
B Lucius
C Jonathan
D Sean

7

WHICH VILLAIN USES THE TUNNELER?

A Bomb Voyage
B Syndrome
C The Underminer
D The Procrastinator

8

WHICH SUPER HELPS ELASTIGIRL GET IN EVELYN'S PLANE?

A Krushauer
B Brick
C He-lectrix
D Voyd

9

WHAT IS SYNDROME DEFEATED BY?

A His cape
B His rocket boots
C His remote-control gloves
D His robots

10

WHICH OF THESE IS **NOT** ONE OF JACK-JACK'S POWERS?

A Shape-shifting
B Super speed
C Teleportation
D Replication

DASH'S TOP 10 INCREDIBLE MOMENTS

10 He saves Violet from the fireball in the cave.

9 When his mom shuts her bedroom door, he's immediately outside looking in the window.

8 He uses his fast kicks to power a boat.

ACTUALLY, HIS MOM WAS THE BOAT.

7 He finishes and understands his math homework.

6 He brings his dad back onto the ship just in time.

MR. INCREDIBLE TRUSTS DASH WITH HIS LIFE.

5 He discovers the Incredibile's voice command.

4 He's okay with coming in second place at his track meet.

HE'LL DO WHATEVER IT TAKES TO KEEP HIS FAMILY'S SECRET!

3 He outruns the Velocipods in the jungle.

2 He saves his siblings when he uses the Incredibile remote to escape.

1 HE RUNS ACROSS WATER. EVEN HE IS SURPRISED BY THAT!

TOP 10 TOOLS OF A SUPER VILLAIN

10 Equipment that causes lots of destruction or even explosions

9 A good monologue

VILLAINS LOVE MONOLOGUING!

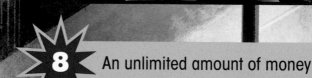

8 An unlimited amount of money

ALL THAT SUPER TECH IS EXPENSIVE!

7 An incredibly cool vehicle, usually with an escape pod

6 A catchy motto

"WHEN EVERYONE IS SUPER, NO ONE WILL BE."
—SYNDROME

5 Equipment for holding your enemies

THE BEST SUPER VILLAINS WAIT TO MONOLOGUE UNTIL THE HERO IS TRAPPED.

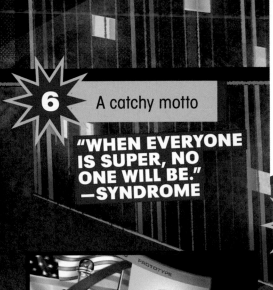

4 A control room with a wall-size screen

3 A convincing disguise

2 A clever name like Bomb Voyage, the Screenslaver, or the Underminer

1 A SECRET LAIR

JACK-JACK'S TOP 10 INCREDIBLE MOMENTS

10 He plays keep-away with the babysitter.

IS IT CHEATING IF YOU CAN FLOAT THROUGH WALLS?

9 Syndrome almost drops him when he turns to heavy metal.

8 Any time he teleports.

HE MUST BE THE BEST PEEKABOO PLAYER.

7

He becomes a sticky goo ball.

BABIES ARE MESSY, BUT JACK-JACK BRINGS IT TO ANOTHER LEVEL.

6

He saves his mom
from the Screenslaver.

**GOODBYE,
HYPNO-GOGGLES!**

5 He gets on Edna's good
side by copying her look.

4 He traps the raccoon
all by himself.

3 Any time he sneezes.

**WATCH OUT FOR LASER BEAMS,
FIREBALLS, AND LIGHTNING BOLTS!**

2 He turns into a monster
when he wants a cookie.

1

EVERY TIME
HE GIGGLES.

CUTEST LAUGH EVER!

TOP 10 REASONS EDNA IS INCREDIBLE

10 She's a famous fashion designer.

BUT SHE'S NOT IMPRESSED WITH SUPERMODELS.

9 She loves chatting with Supers, especially Elastigirl.

8 She forbids capes.

SHE'S LEARNED FROM HER MISTAKES.

7 She has an impressive security system.

6

She tells people exactly how she feels.

5

Her house is as fashionable as she is.

IT ALSO CONTAINS HER SUPER HIGH-TECH LAB!

4

She may be short, but she can intimidate even the toughest Super.

3

She's a wonderful babysitter.

2

She engineers amazing technology in fabulous Supersuits.

1

SHE IS A CREATIVE PROBLEM SOLVER.

TOP 10 SUPER POWERS YOU CAN HAVE

10 **COURAGE**

Heroes don't let their fears stop them.

9 **OPTIMISM**

Heroes never give up hope.

8 **CURIOSITY**

Heroes never stop learning.

7 **HONOR**

Heroes work for the greater good.

6
TRUSTWORTHINESS
Heroes are dependable.

5
HELPFULNESS
Heroes want to be useful.

4
RESOURCEFULNESS
Heroes solve problems in creative ways.

3
PERSISTENCE
Heroes don't give up if something goes wrong.

2
COOPERATION
Heroes need to work well with others.

1
COMPASSION
Heroes care about others.

MAKE YOUR OWN
INCREDIBLES TOP 10!

IT'S TIME TO PICK *YOUR* FAVORITES. Make a copy of the blank list on the next page. Don't agree with the lists in this book? Change them. Or make a new list, such as

- **THE TOP 10 REASONS TO INVITE THE INCREDIBLES TO YOUR BIRTHDAY PARTY**

- **JACK-JACK'S TOP 10 SUPER POWERS**

Use your super list-making skills to create some incredible lists of your own!

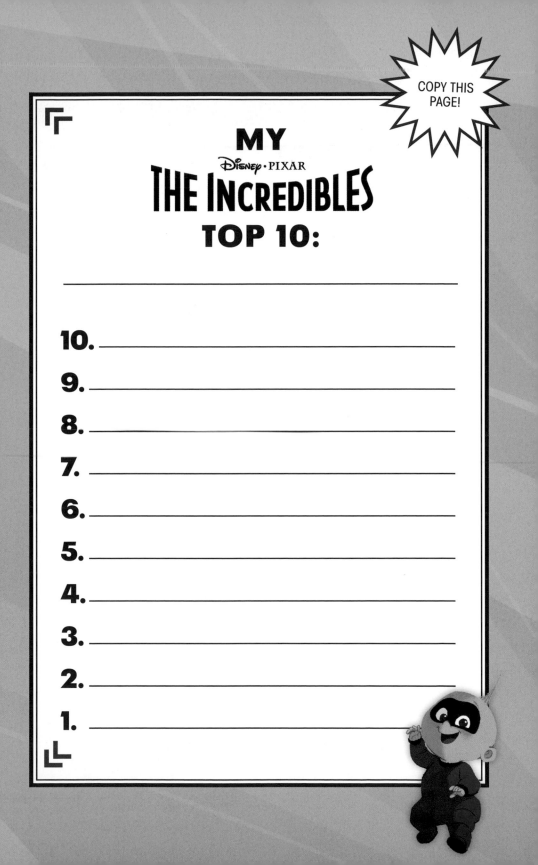

COPY THIS PAGE!

MY
Disney·PIXAR
THE INCREDIBLES
TOP 10:

10. _____

9. _____

8. _____

7. _____

6. _____

5. _____

4. _____

3. _____

2. _____

1. _____

TO LEARN MORE

Books

Boothroyd, Jennifer. *How to Be a Hero: Responsibility with the Incredibles*. Minneapolis: Lerner Publications, 2019.
Learn what it takes to be a hero from everyone's favorite crime-fighting family, the Incredibles. Discover how responsibility is an important key to a hero's success.

Disney. *The Incredi-Files.* New York: Penguin Random House, 2018.
This guidebook gives details on all the characters and vehicles from the world of the Incredibles.

Websites

Disney Movies: *Incredibles 2*
https://movies.disney.com/incredibles-2
Dive into *Incredibles 2*. Download activities, get caught up on movie news, and more.

Disney Movies: *The Incredibles*
http://movies.disney.com/the-incredibles
Explore the world of *The Incredibles*.
Watch a video clip from the movie.
Play a game with Dash or Frozone.
Learn more about the characters
by reading their bios.

3386